DATA LITERACY for Kids

written & illustrated by Kathleen Yu

AUTHOR'S NOTE

In today's data-driven world, understanding and interpreting data is a vital skill in all aspects of life. This book is dedicated towards spreading data literacy among young students, and inspiring them to use data to solve problems, make informed decisions, and create a positive impact.

Meet **LILY**

a data expert.

MAX is her best friend,
but he doesn't know anything about data.

Are you ready to
learn all about data?

Yes! Let's do this!

Wait...what is data?

Imagine you have a big toy box full of different toys.

Each toy is like a piece of data.

Data is a collection of information, just like a collection of toys, that helps people make decisions and predictions.

Data is also like puzzle pieces.

Each puzzle piece is different, but when you put them all together...

...you get one

big picture!

Data is everywhere, and we use it everyday!

We use data when we count things,

keep track of scores,

and even to predict the weather!

Is data only numbers?

No, data can be in the form of anything!

Data can be words,

Favorite Books
- Charlotte's Web
- Harry Potter
- The Giving Tree
- Pete the Cat

pictures,

and even sounds!

But wait, how and where do you get data?

Great question! Let's talk about...

DATA COLLECTION

Let's say that we want to find out if cheese, pepperoni, or veggie pizza is the most popular flavor at school.

One way we can do this is by using a survey. A survey is when you ask people questions to gather information.

These are the results of a survey on a mix of 40 students and teachers.

Pizza Flavors

	Students	Teachers
Cheese	2	11
Pepperoni	1	9
Veggie	0	20

However, there's a problem with this data. Do you know what it is?

Hmm...wait a second. There are more teachers surveyed than students!

That's right! 40 teachers were surveyed while only 3 students were surveyed.

From this survey, veggie pizza would be the most popular.

 But that's not true! Veggie pizza is definitely NOT the most popular.

That's why when we collect data, it is important to have a representative sample.

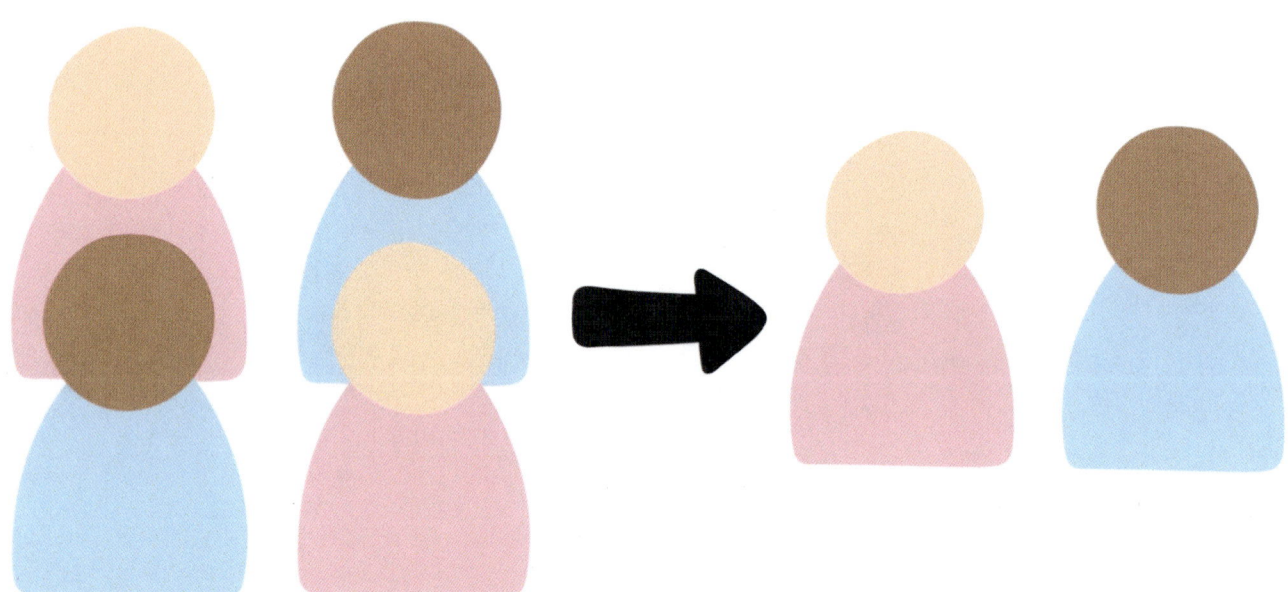

A representative sample is exactly what it sounds like! It means that the sample represents the entire group it was taken from.

Let's say that half of the school population are students, and the other half are teachers.

This means that...

We must collect data from an equal number of students and teachers.

These are the results of a new survey.

Pizza Flavors

	Students	Teachers
Cheese	21	11
Pepperoni	18	9
Veggie	1	20

Here, 40 students and 40 teachers were surveyed.

By collecting data from a representative sample, our data is more reliable and accurate.

I knew cheese was the most popular flavor!

Now that you know what data is and how to collect it, let's take a look at...

DATA VISUALIZATIONS

What are data visualizations?

Data visualizations tell a story and help us find patterns and trends in data.

There are many types of data visualizations.

Let's go over some of them!

First, let's look at a...

TALLY CHART

This simple tally chart is a data visualization.

It tells us how many people like each ice cream flavor by the number of tallies.

We can see that vanilla is the most popular,

and strawberry is the least popular.

Tally charts are so cool! I love chocolate the best though.

Now, let's take a look at another visualization called a...

PIE CHART

Pie charts look like a sliced pie!

And a pizza!

That's right! I'm going to explain a pie chart using a list of our friends' favorite colors.

Favorite Colors
- Blue: Mary, Bob, Sue, Jack
- Red: Max
- Pink: Lily
- Green: Brian, Claire

Match the Data:

which tally chart represents the data?

Blue: | | | |
Red: |
Pink: |
Green: | |

Blue: ||||
Red:
Pink: | |
Green: |

Blue: | |
Red: |
Pink: | |
Green: | |

Blue: |
Red: | | |
Pink: | | |
Green: |

Answer: The blue one!

This pie chart is divided into slices of different sizes.

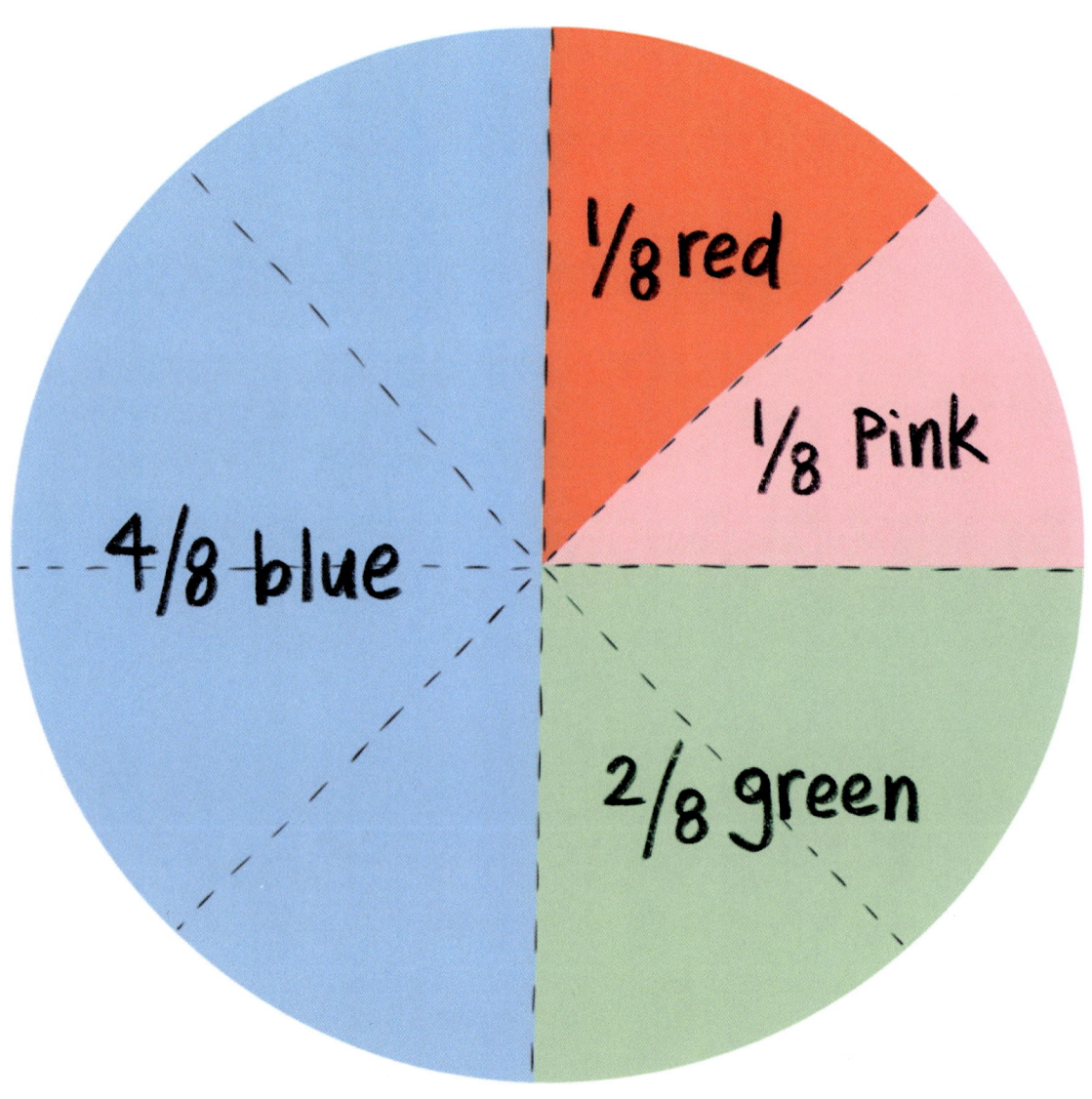

The size of each slice shows how popular each color is.

Does this mean that the most popular color is blue since it has the biggest slice?

That's right!

$$\frac{1}{2} \quad \frac{7}{8} \quad \frac{9}{10}$$

Pie charts also represent fractions.

The entire pie represents all of the data, just like the denominator of a fraction...

...and each slice represents a portion of the data, just like the numerator of a fraction.

Pie charts are a great way to see proportions and percentages.

Now, let's take a look at...

BAR GRAPHS

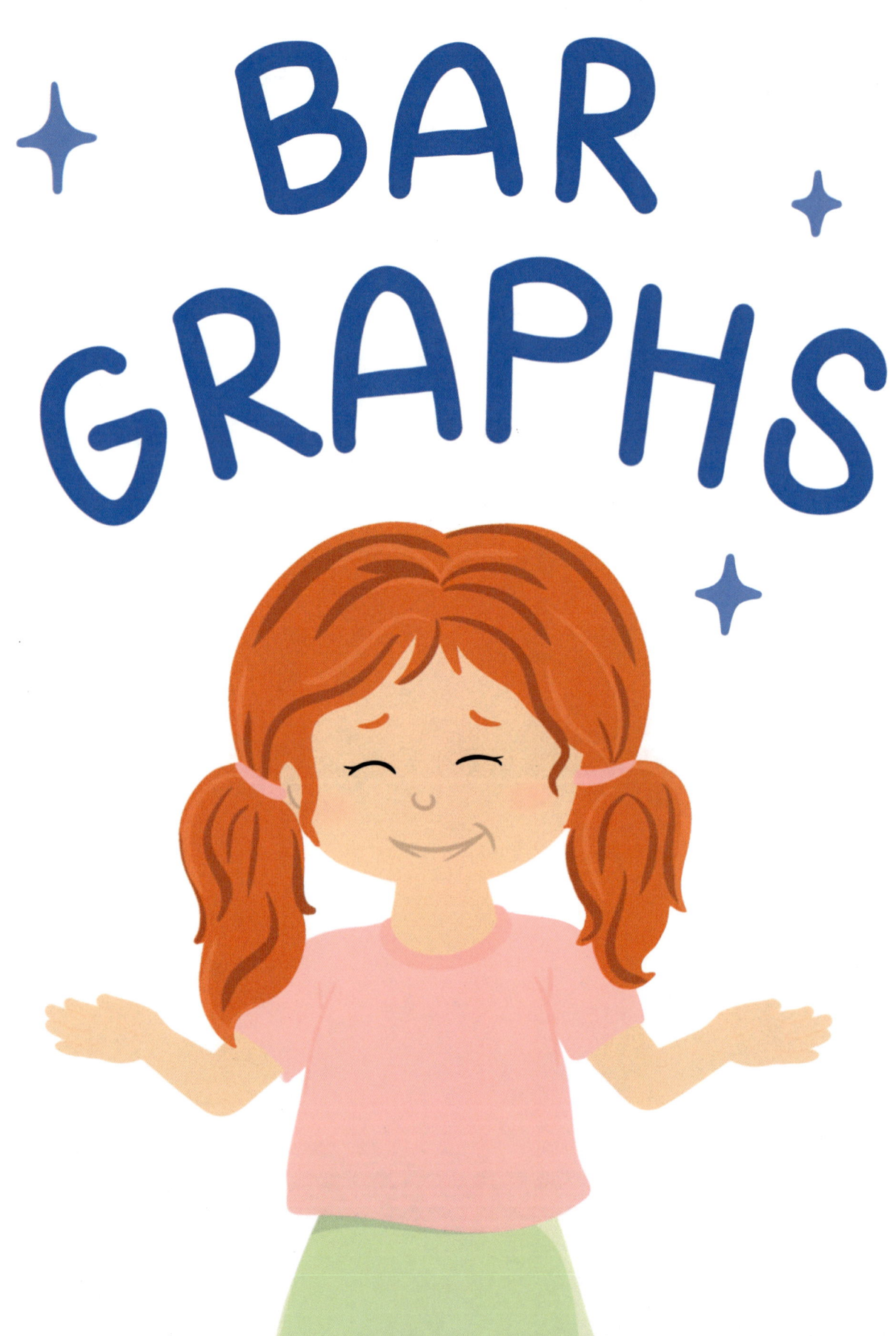

Imagine a stack of toy blocks.

The more blocks there are, the higher the tower.

Each block is like a piece of data...

...and each tower is like a bar on a bar graph.

Can you explain using pets?

Great idea! Here's a tally chart of favorite pets.

Favorite Pets
- Dogs: |||| |||
- Birds: ||
- Cats: |||| ||
- Fish: ||||

In this bar graph, each bar represents a type of pet.

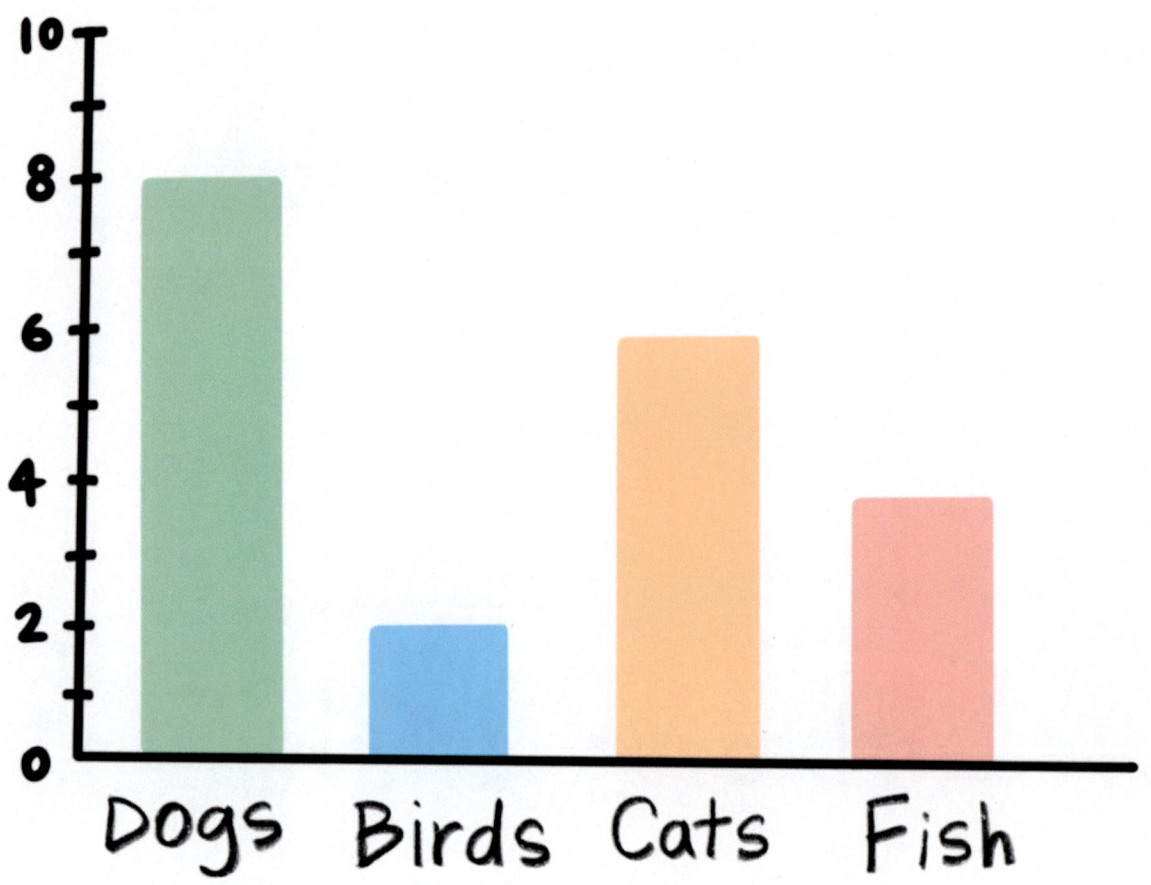

The height of each bar represents the number of tally marks for each pet.

Is the height of a bar in a bar graph similar to the size of a slice in a pie chart?

Exactly! Both are different ways to help us picture data.

Try It Yourself:

Which pet is most popular?

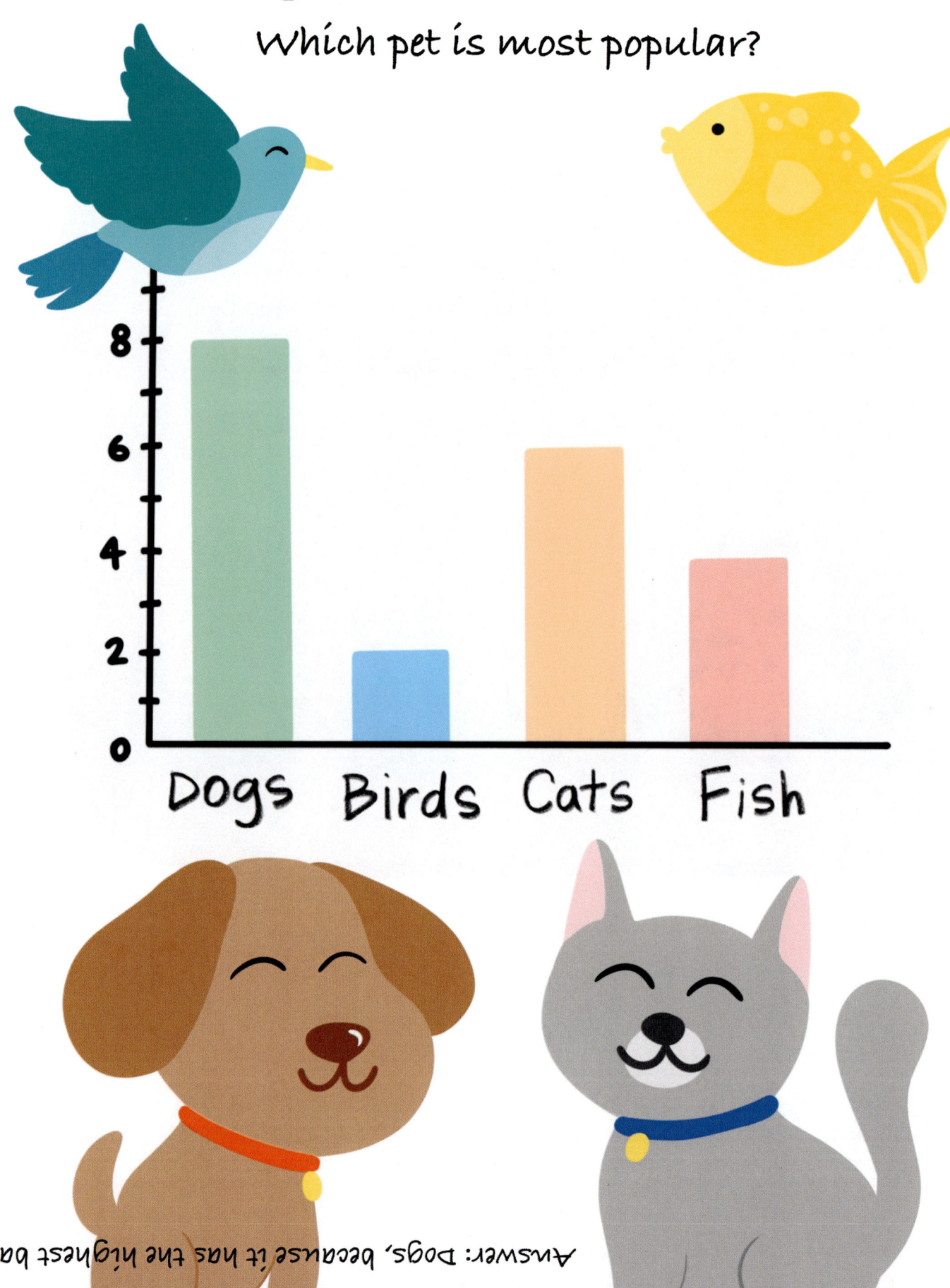

Answer: Dogs, because it has the highest bar!

You're getting closer to becoming a data expert!

Let's learn a more challenging graph now...

the SCATTERPLOT

Let's look at an example.

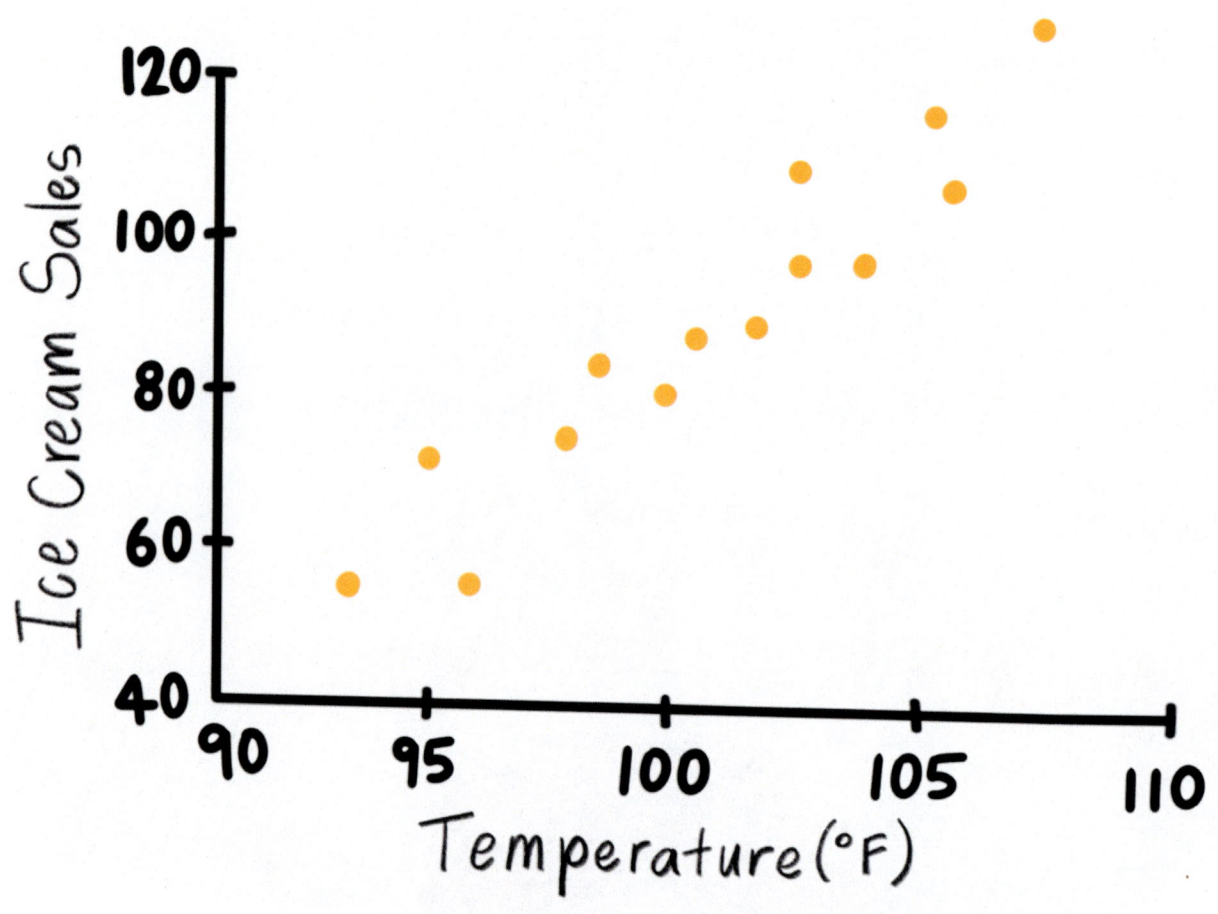

Wow, there's so many dots!

Scatterplots help us find patterns between two variables.

Wait...what's a variable?

Think of the toy box again.

Just like how a toy box can store different toys, a variable is a letter, symbol, or word that can store different data values.

So... a toy box is like a variable, and the toys in the toy box are like data values?

Yes! The data values a variable stores can change just like how toys in a toy box can be switched.

Pop Quiz:

What are the two variables in this scatterplot?

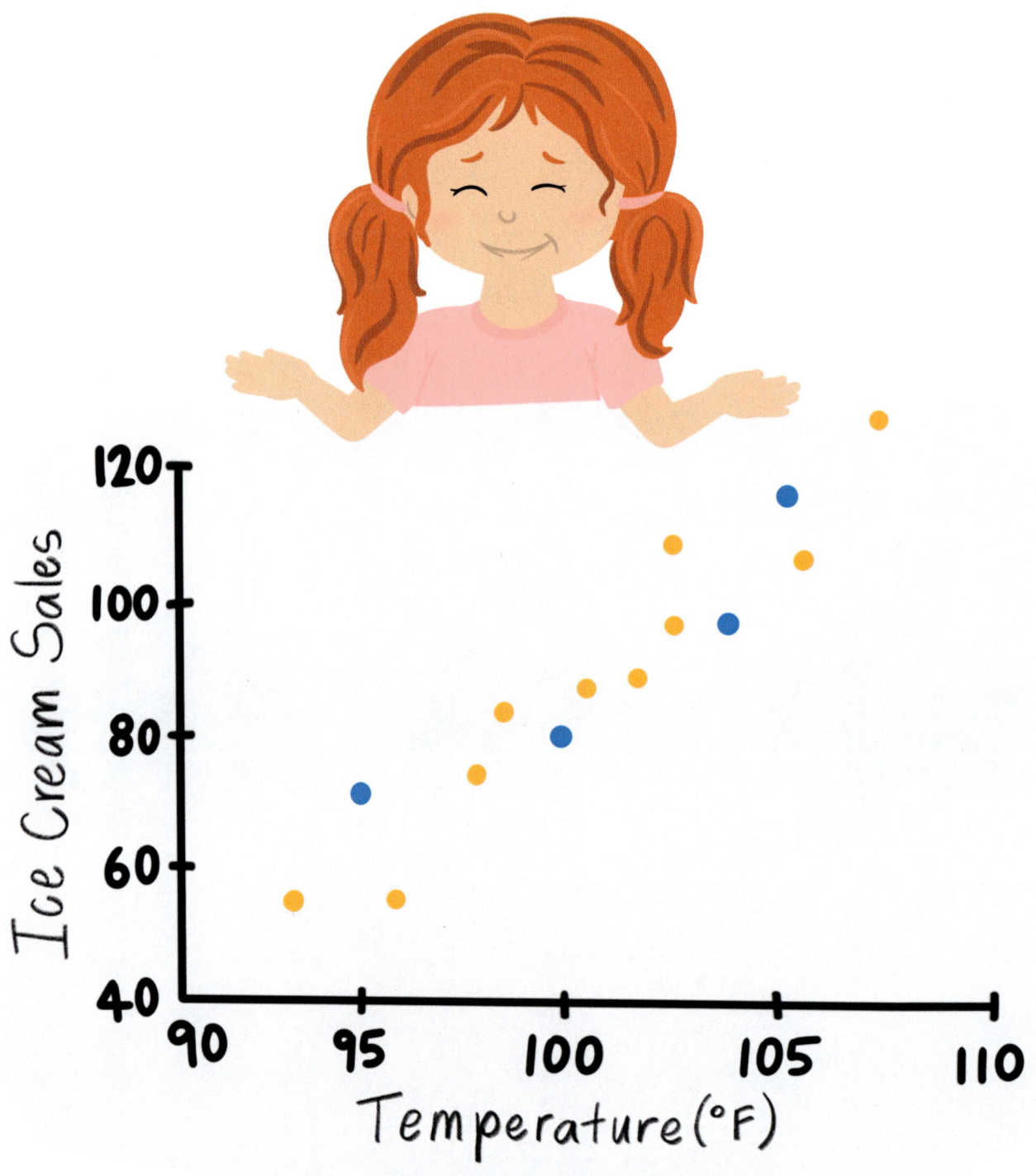

Answer: 1. Temperature 2. Ice Cream Sales

Now back to our scatterplot.

Here is the data for the blue dots on the scatterplot.

	Temperature	Sales
1.	95°	70
2.	100°	80
3.	104°	95
4.	105°	115

If you look closely, what do you notice about the dots on the scatterplot?

Hmm...the dots seem to be in the shape of a line.

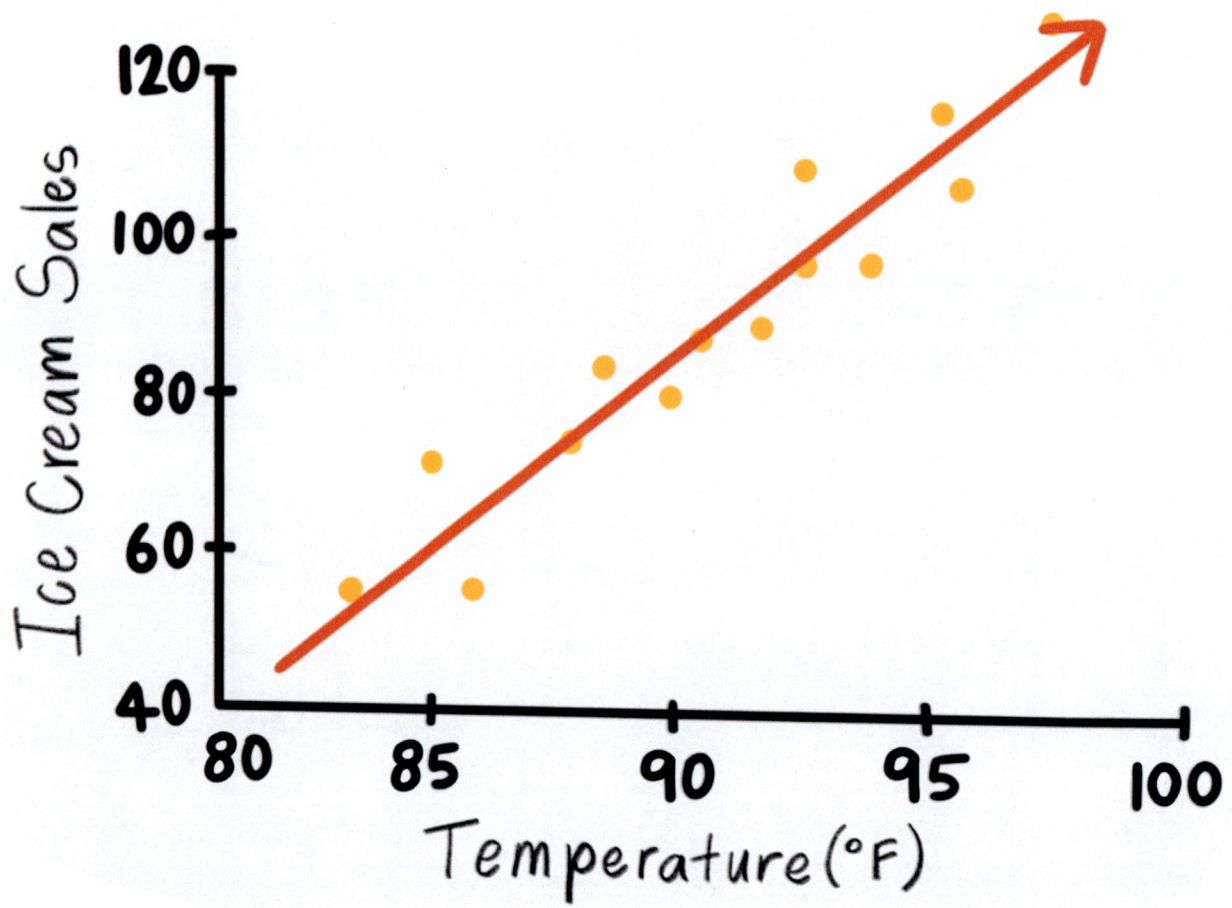

Because the line is pointing upwards, the temperature outside and the number of ice creams eaten have a positive relationship.

This means that when it is hotter outside, more people buy ice cream.

So, a positive relationship means that as the temperature increases, the number of ice cream sales also increases, right?

Exactly! More people will buy ice cream when it's hotter outside!

Sometimes, the dots in a scatterplot can form a line that points downwards.

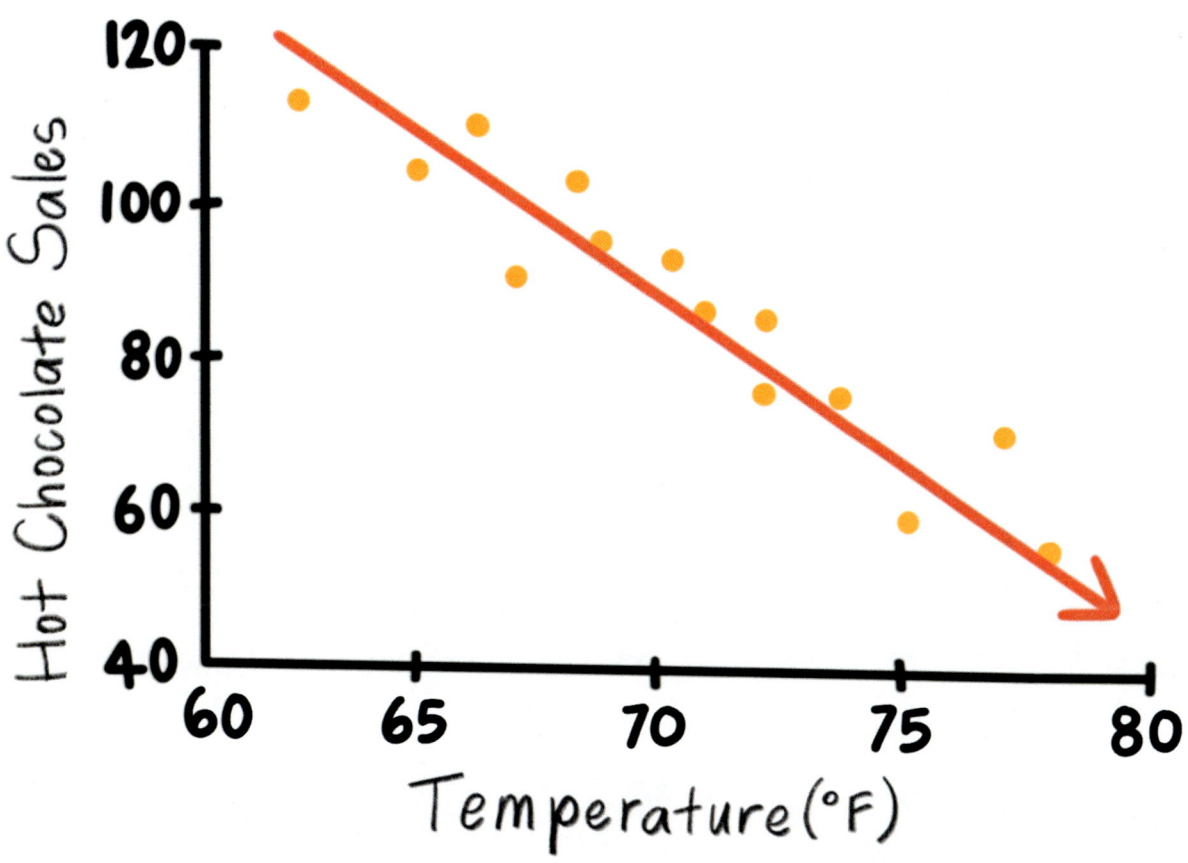

This means that there is a negative relationship between the two variables.

Sometimes, the dots can also be completely random.

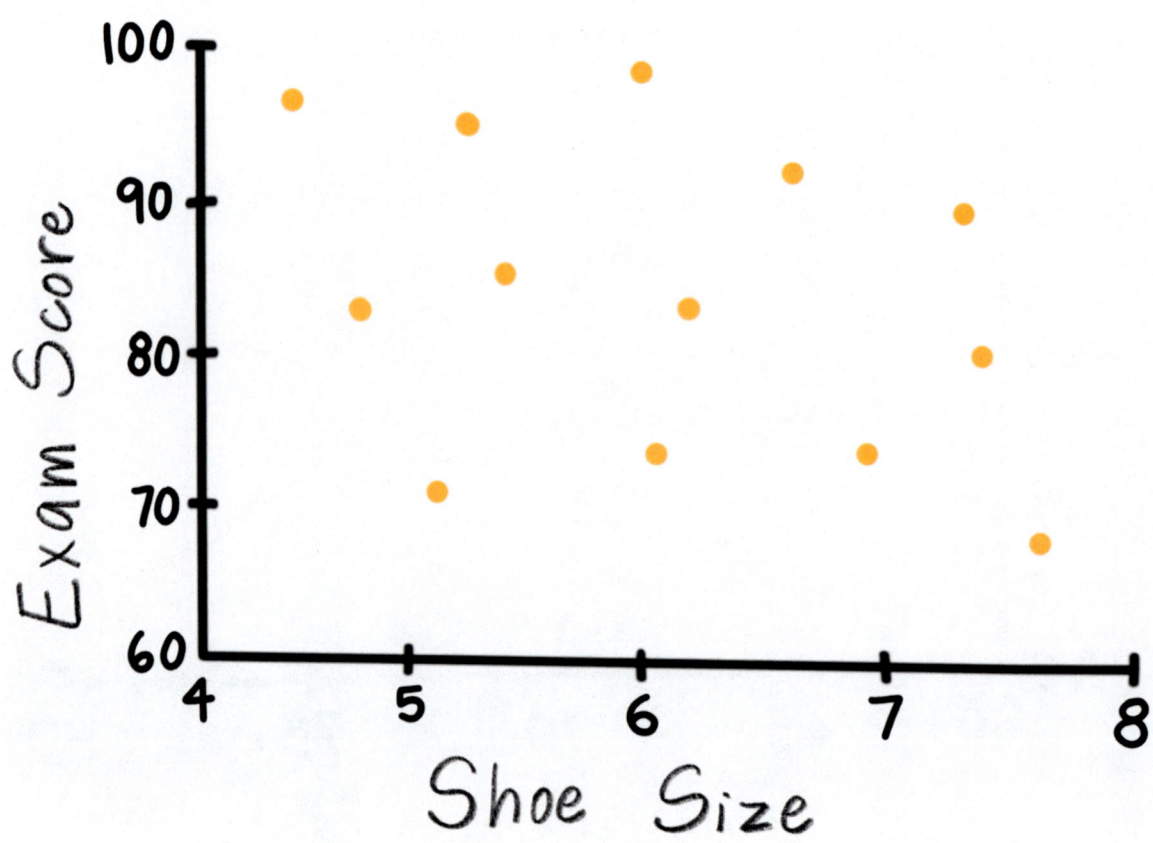

This means that there is no relationship between the two variables.

Ohhh...that makes sense because someone's shoe size and exam score are unrelated.

Yes! Scatter plots are great data visualizations because they clearly show the trend and relationship between 2 variables.

I feel like a data expert already!

You've already learned 3 of the most common data visualizations.

Keep it up!

Remember the survey we conducted earlier on the most popular pizza flavor at school?

Yes, I do!

Let's use everything we've learned to create data visualizations with the data!

As a reminder, here is the data.

40 students and 40 teachers were surveyed. Cheese pizza was the winner because it had the highest number of votes.

This is a pie chart of the data.

From this pie chart, we can clearly see the popularity of each flavor.

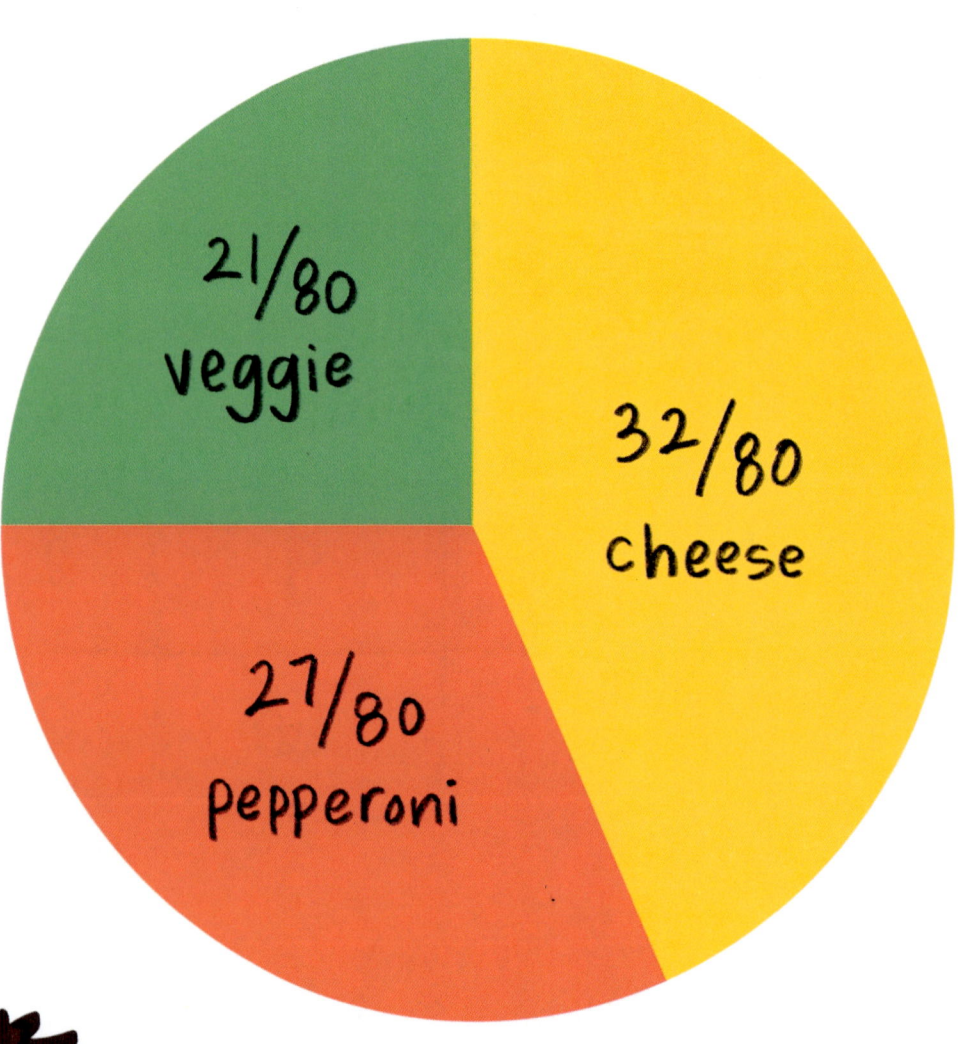

Remember, the size of each slice represents the proportion of the whole!

Your Turn:

Which bar graph matches the data?

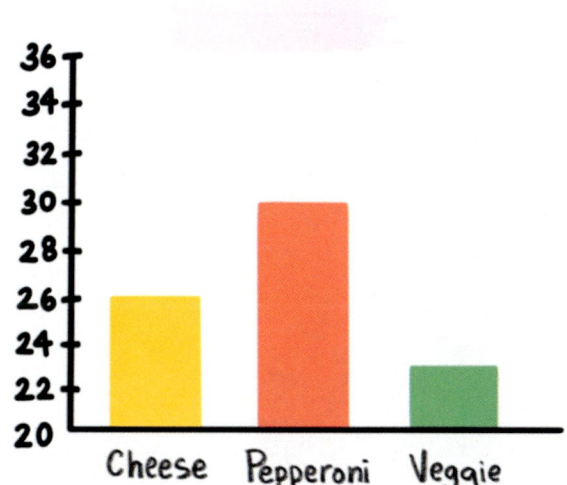

Answer: The graph with the blue tape.

Now that we have 2 data visualizations, how can we use them?

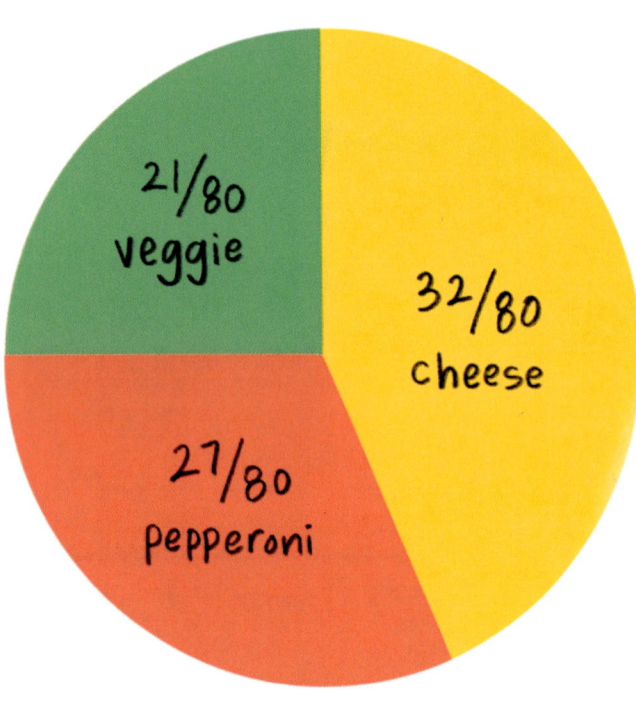

We can share this pie chart and bar graph with the school!

Then, the school can use our data and these visualizations to decide which pizza flavor to sell more of.

Since cheese is the most popular, the school can sell more cheese pizza in the cafeteria!

That's how you communicate with data
and use it to make decisions.

I feel like a data expert now!

Now, you can use your data skills to find patterns, solve problems, and help others.

Data is so cool! I'm going to use my new data skills everyday.

Thank you, Lily!

Now, embrace the power of data and let your imagination

SOAR!

Made in the USA
Coppell, TX
15 August 2023